AFTERLIFE
CONNECTIONS
True Stories That Prove That Love Never Dies

Blair Robertson

Aberdeenshire Publishing

PHOENIX, ARIZONA

Afterlife Connections
Blair Robertson
Copyright (c) 2015 by Blair Robertson

Aberdeenshire Publishing
Box 1306
Litchfield Park, Arizona 85340

For my daughter, Beth

"Love never dies."

—BLAIR ROBERTSON

CONTENTS

Introduction

Holidays such as Christmas, Thanksgiving, New Year's and Valentine's Day are especially painful. Especially if they are the first alone. Of course other dates just birthdays, anniversaries, etc. are equally as hard.

The purpose of this book is to remind you that love never dies. It is true that we all will eventually pass away physically, but our soul or spirit continues.

This book was written for you by people like you for one purpose and goal: to help make you aware that your loved ones are near, and they're showing you signs on a regular basis.

The problem is most people don't recognize the signs. In the companion book to this one called **Afterlife: 3 Easy Ways To Connect And Communicate With Your Deceased Loved Ones**, I reveal the five signs that our loved ones often show us. (The book is free, and I urge you get it and read it.)

Not all signs are signs! It's important to know and understand the difference between what are real signs and what are not. It becomes very easy when you understand the differences! But the most important thing is once you do recognize differences you'll start seeing more signs. You'll learn how to tune-in, and your loved ones will lovingly share more.

As you might imagine over the past 30-years, I've heard thousands of stories of people who have made connections with their loved ones on the other side. I received emails, Facebook posts, blog posts and first-hand stories from people at my events.

In today's busy world, these stories quickly get lost. So this book was written at the request of people like you asked me to share stories.

Here they are! I hope you like them, and I hope that they inspire you. But most of all it's my hearts desire to convey to you that love never dies.

Blair Robertson

P.S. While these stories are true, we have changed names and other identifiers for privacy reasons. We have edited as lightly as possible for clarity. I'm profoundly grateful to everyone whoever has shared a story, regardless if included or not. Every story shared has the power to heal. Namaste.

From A Skeptic To A Believer

Mum lost her life on Christmas of 2002. My parents had borne me in their forties and despite the fact that I could see that she was growing old, I never once thought of her death. To me, mum would always be around. I loved her with all my heart and we spoke on the phone every day and met several times a week.

She was strong and did everything for herself, from cleaning to cooking. I had gently hinted that she should come and live with us. She looked at me, horrified. Why would she invade our space when she was fit and healthy and able to care for herself? My reason for wanting her close to me was that I could see that chores that used to take her a short time now took hours.

As I saw it, I would take over the cooking and cleaning and she wouldn't have to lift a finger. It would have been against mum's nature to sit back and let someone else care for her. She valued her independence and though her gait was slow, she still enjoyed her shopping and her walk to the park.

Her death therefore came as a shock to me and I thought of her constantly. I missed her with an intensity that left my body weak. I had never given much thought to what happens after death. I suppose to me, death was final. After mum had died however, I wished that I could see her one more time but I knew that it wasn't possible.

Christmas approached and I couldn't summon up the joy that I approached it in the previous years. Our family loved Christmas, the only time that mum agreed to sleep over at our house. Christmas Eve usually found us preparing meals and chatting happily in the kitchen. Mum would have her white apron on and be giving orders to the rest of us.

In 2002, mum was getting ready for me to pick her up at her house for the two nights that she would be with us. We had arranged that I would pick her up at eleven in the morning. I drove to her house at just about eleven and when I rang the doorbell, there was no answer. Puzzled, I went round to the back and peered in through the kitchen window.

Mum was lying on the floor of the kitchen, her body still. She was fastidious about keeping the doors locked up and even as I tried the back door, I knew it would be locked from the inside. I banged the window frantically but she did not respond. I called out to her until my voice got hoarse and then finally I called the paramedics.

I was a bundle of nerves by then. They broke the door and I rushed to mum's side.

She was gone. Her body was still warm and her face arranged into a small smile as though she was engrossed in a sweet dream. I wrapped my hands around myself and shivered in my warm winter coat. It took me a while to take in that mum was gone and she wasn't coming back.

Christmas Eve was, therefore, a terrible day for me and I distracted myself from thoughts of mum by watching a couple of films. When the films were over, I dragged myself to the kitchen to prepare vegetables to accompany our dinner. More than any other day before that, mum's presence was all around me as I cooked.

I imagined her beside me dicing onions and tomatoes and darting between the kitchen and the fridge. I hoped the next couple of days would fly by fast as I didn't know how I would get through them. Mum especially loved it when we exchanged presents and her laugh would ring throughout the house.

My daughter and the dog were upstairs and the room was silent. I heard a noise from the living room and I went to check. There was no one, my daughter and the dog were still upstairs. I discarded it from my mind. I opened the fridge. It felt frigid, colder than normal. I turned my head and saw mum coming towards me.

I froze. She seemed to float in the air as I couldn't see her feet. Her face was not very clear but there was no doubt that the figure in front of me was mum. I can't recall the details of her dress but it was what she would normally wear when she was alive. I panicked. I took the few steps across the kitchen to the counter top.

I stood stiffly, my hands gripping the edges of the worktop. Then a thought crossed my mind. What if it wasn't mum? I said out aloud: 'Thank you for coming I have seen you, goodbye.'

The figure retreated and when I looked into the living room, she was gone. It was six in the evening and I hadn't been asleep or day dreaming. I know that was mum and I now wish that I had spoken to her some more. But for someone who hadn't given much weight to loved ones living on after their death, my brain had frozen that evening, unable to comprehend that mum who had passed on was now standing in front of me.

I'm now a firm believer from firsthand experience that our loved ones never truly leave us. I live with the hope that mum will visit me again and this time I'll be better prepared. I'm grateful for that experience, though because it opened my eyes and my heart to believing in life after death. It's a comforting thought to know that we'll be together again.

These days, I keep my ears and my eyes open just in case mum makes another appearance. When she does, I'll tell her something more personal and I'll tell her that I'm now at peace, knowing that she is too.

A Savior From Beyond

My husband Edwin passed on and though I missed him terribly, I had to stay strong to watch over our youngest son who had Down's syndrome. It overwhelmed me sometimes having to take care of him by myself. Edwin and our son James had been very close and had a special connection. James took his dad's death hard. He retreated into himself and did not speak after his father passed on.

He had been verbal before that and could express his thoughts and wishes albeit in awkward sentences. It was painful to watch his blank facial expression and his mouth tightly shut. I worried over what was going on in his mind. He never asked for anything and just kept to himself. We trudged through the days and my grief lifted somewhat.

Edwin had retired from his job three years before his death. He and James spent all their days together. They planned each day with military precision. They would do the garden in the morning, clean the car in the afternoon and do other odd jobs around the house together. Edwin took him on walks to the park and the stores. They enjoyed each other's company and chatted throughout the day.

His dad's passing left a big gap in James's life. Suddenly his dad was not there to keep him occupied throughout the day and to chat to him. I don't know how much of death that James understood, but it probably pained him that his dad could not be with him. It would have been easier on me if James had spoken and told me what he was thinking and feeling.

I knew that it would be hard on James but I hadn't known how grief stricken he would be. He looked at his dad's framed pictures sadly and it broke my heart. I tried to coax him to take walks with me but he didn't want to, preferring to be around the house. No matter how much I tried, I couldn't comfort him. I attempted to keep myself cheerful throughout the day and that too took its toll. By night time, my brain would be exhausted from the strain of staying happy for James's sake. I never indulged on my grief. James needed me to provide a semblance of normality even though the person who had been the center of his life was gone.

He did agree to go with me to Edwin's grave to lay some fresh flowers but that was just about it. I spoke to him about Edwin but he gave no indication of understanding what I said. On my part, I had some good days and some bad days. I worried about James's inability to speak. What if he needed help, what would happen when he couldn't verbalize it? There was not much that I could do. Only time would heal his grief.

One day, we went to bed at our usual time. I'm known to sleep undisturbed throughout the night. Edwin had teased me often that the only thing that would arouse me from sleep was the ringing doorbell or a phone call. I said goodnight to James and went to my room. He seemed alright, tucked into his blankets and ready to sleep.

As usual, I fell asleep immediately my head touched the pillow. A couple of hours later, the doorbell rang. Thinking that my imagination was playing tricks on me, I turned and slept on. Seconds later, it rang again, clearly and loudly. I woke up wondering who would be coming to the house at that time of night.

I rubbed my eyes and got up from a bed. I opened the door and there was no one there. Still sleepy, I shrugged, closed it and made my way back to my bedroom. I checked on James expecting to find him asleep in bed. Instead, he was huddled in a corner of his room, looking scared.

I went into his room to coax him back to bed. I picked up the blanket by his bed and it burst into flames.

I jumped back in fright. Underneath the blanket was the lamp that had started the fire. Already, the carpet had been burned through and the fire was consuming the floor underneath. I took James and we hurried out of the room.

The fire department arrived soon after and thankfully they got the fire under control. They handed me a picture frame with a picture of Edwin. The wooden frame had been burnt and the glass partially destroyed but the picture was intact. I looked at the photo, and Edwin seemed to be looking straight at me, smiling.

The firefighters said that the only reason James's bed had not gone up in flames was because the picture frame and the glass had acted as buffers between the blanket and the lamp. The picture of Edwin usually sat on top of the chest of drawers. James had probably brought it to his bedside to feel closer to his dad.

Had the doorbell not rung, I would not have woken up to check on James. After bidding each other goodnight, we both finally slept through the night. I know that Edwin had rung the bell that night, knowing that it was the only way to alert me to the danger that lurked in our son's room. Had the phone rang, I would not have walked past James's room and Edwin knew that. My other children and I know without a shadow of a doubt that Edwin had saved us that night.

Since then, my feelings of being overwhelmed have disappeared. I know that I don't watch over James alone, as Edwin is right there with me. Slowly by slowly, James is becoming verbal again and he is slowly coming to terms with his dad's passing. I feel Edwin's presence with us every day, and I know whenever we need him, he'll be right there with us, protecting us from harm.

Just One More Time

It was 1997, and I was recovering from a long illness and decided it would be a good idea to stay at my sister's house in Orange County. Being sick for a long time has a way of making you feel very vulnerable and need of comfort. I had been a grown woman for a long time, but I still longed for my mother's care and nurturing love, especially when I was feeling so bad physically. After staying with my sister, it was time to return to West Hollywood and my husband and son. My sister and I are very close, and she was a blessing to have with me during my healing process, but I was longing to be back home with my family.

Although I was still on oxygen, I felt well enough to drive myself home to West Hollywood. However, the hour and a half trip seemed long, leaving me feel more physically uncomfortable than I had anticipated. The cars and the scenery seemed to pass by me in a daze, and the road stretched out long and endlessly before me. During the drive from Orange County to Los Angeles, I felt lost in reverie, thinking of my illness, my life and my mother who had passed away quite some time ago.

So many emotions were coming to the surface, and I felt sad and depressed over everything.

I was so relieved when I finally arrived home. We had lived in this house for a few years now and it seemed like a perfect fit for our family. I knew no one was home as I opened the door and quickly dropped my things on the floor. Exhausted after the long drive, sat down on the couch to rest, thinking about everything that had happened recently with my mom, my life, my health, and I felt my eyes welling up with tears.

I said out loud to myself with great longing, "I wish I could talk to my mom just one more time!" At that moment the phone rang and I picked it up. An elderly woman on the other line said, "Carol, is that you?" I answered yes. She said, "This is your mother". I completely broke down, started crying and said, "You must have the wrong number!" With her apologies, we both hung up. I sat there trying to process what had just happened feeling confused and emotional.

A few minutes later, the phone rang again and of course I answered. The same elderly lady said, "Carol, is that you? This is your mother." I could barely get the words out I was crying so much, but I managed to tell her that she must have the wrong number and asked for her to repeat the number that she was dialing. Then- with what seemed like slow motion- she repeated the phone number that we had had for the last few years. At that point, I completely lost it. I was in total shock. I curled up on the cough, wrapped my arms around my bent knees, lowered my head and bawled for what seemed like hours.

My face wet with tears, my eyes swollen and my nose red, my husband and son rushed through the front door in anticipation of our long awaited reunion, and saw me sitting there crying inconsolably. Their beautiful smiling faces dropped, imagining something terrible had happened to me as I must have looked like a total mess. With their loving warmth, I explained how I had been feeling especially low and missing my mother. They, like myself, were in total shock with the phone calls I had received from a lovely older lady who had been attempting to call her daughter, just at the time I had willed my mother to talk with me.   We knew then and still know today, that my mom did contact me after all. What a wonderful, unforgettable experience of love reaching out from the other side.

King Of My Heart

It was July 7th, 2012, a scorching summer day where the sun seemed to target its hot rays directly on me like a spotlight on the stage. I was running an errand at the post office, mailing some important letters for my business. I felt proud of myself that after such a short amount of time I was getting back into the swing of things and doing my best to handle the routine tasks of life. My fiancée had passed away in March from cancer, and we had spent 16 months of love and happiness together. He was the man that I had always dreamed I would meet, but sadly our time was cut short. He was my soul mate and my best friend, and I had looked forward to spending a lifetime with him.

As I was walking into the post office, I noticed a beautiful butterfly circling over a flower bed of daisies. The deep golden orange of its wings matched the flower petals and the dark brown spots echoed the chocolate colored centers of each delicate daisy. I gazed at it for a few seconds and as if it recognized me, suddenly turned and glided in my direction and hovered in front of me. For whatever reason, I felt this butterfly was of the male gender. I looked up and cooed as if I knew him. I told him I had to go in and mail my letters. I didn't want to leave him but the office was about to close. At this, he fluttered back to the flower bed as if he understood my every word.

As I was waiting in line at the post office I felt anxious and preoccupied. I wanted to return to the butterfly and hoped that it would still be there. It didn't feel like just a butterfly; it felt like an intimate friend that I wanted to reunite with. When I walked outside the sun harshly hit my eyes and I wondered if my butterfly would still be there. I felt sure that the butterfly was close by because I had felt this strong connection, so I patiently waited by my car. Within a minute I saw him fluttering his beautiful golden wings over the yellow daisies. He was so camouflaged by the daisies that it was initially hard to see him.

I called to him in my mind. He fluttered back to me and hovered over my head suspended in mid-air the way that hummingbirds seem to do. I gazed up at him, taking in his beauty that all butterflies have, but this "Monarch" was extra special. I felt within that I knew him. We seemed to be in telepathic communication and I could feel a resonance between us. It felt as though time stood still and we were suspended at that moment together. I felt this overwhelming desire to reach up and bring him home with me, as I didn't want to leave him. My rational mind told me this wasn't possible so. Instead, I looked intently at him and as though my heart had a voice, I told him I had to leave but that I would never forget him.

With that communication, his suspension was over, and I watched him circle above my head one more time, his delicate wings fluttering and cutting through the hot July air. I then watched him with love and deep focus as his large orange spotted wings sailed slowly away on the faint summer breeze and he disappeared into the vast field of grass and wildflowers behind the post office. As I gazed at the flowerbed of daisies, there was not another butterfly in sight. This one seemed destined for our meeting.

Driving off in my car, the tears flowed quickly and steadily, cooling my cheeks that felt scorched from the hot July sun. But I did not wonder at why the tears were flowing or why such incredible emotion had been triggered by this encounter with a butterfly. I knew exactly what it all meant. I had just witnessed a mutual and spiritual meeting of love that once was and will always be. My fiancée and I had 16 months of pure joy together. Like most couples, we had nicknames for each other. He called me his "Angel" and I called him my "King of the butterflies, my Monarch". And so I share this true story of profound significance with you. Love never dies, and our loved ones remain in spirit, continuing to remind us that they are always there, whether in human form or a beautiful butterfly.

Blessings From The Other Side

It was a hot and muggy August day when my son Derek passed away from cardiac arrhythmia in 2011. Just like the heat of the day where it was hard to breathe in the summer heat, I felt like the air had been sucked out of me and my chest felt constricted and tight. He was only 16 years old, and it was an extremely sudden and unexpected event. Who could imagine or ever believe that their child could be taken from them and at such a young age. He had barely lived at all. Of course, I was devastated and to move through each day felt like walking through molasses. I felt heavy and every step felt thick and burdened with grief.

As time passed, I did my best to engage in life. I had been unemployed for over a year and a half due to physical issues and with my job as a nurse there were jobs that I simply couldn't do. As a result, I was having a lot of financial difficulties from not having worked in such a long time. My credit was destroyed, and I had an old car that was beat up and on its last leg. Then a series of events occurred that turned my life around and made it clear to me that my son was with me and was sending blessings from the other side.

First, after my long stretch of unemployment I landed my dream job completely out of the blue. One particular day I was just sitting at my kitchen table drinking my coffee out of my favorite mug that had a zebra on it and said "Nothing is black and white," feeling the warmth of Derek, when I received a call from a staffing agency. The woman at the other end of the line was Stacy, an upbeat young girl with a high-pitched squeaky voice. She said that she thought she had a great fit for me taking care of a young physically challenged girl. The next day I went and met her, and we hit it off immediately. It has been the best job that I have ever had, and she has been a client of mine for over three years. I knew deep in my heart and in my gut that this was Derek, who had helped bring this blessing to me.

The other thing that Derek did for me helped me to get a new car. As I had said, my car was falling apart, and I needed a new car badly. I went to a car dealership and because of my bad credit as a result of being unemployed so long, the finance manager was very doubtful as to whether I could get financing for my new car. He assured me that he would do his best, and to not give up hope. When he finally called me a week later, he said to me, "You must be one lucky woman as I contacted 28 lenders and finally just when I was about to give up hope I got one to say yes!" I felt an incredible feeling of love and warmth wash over my body, and I could feel Derek close to me. There was not doubt in my mind that he was responsible for helping me to get this new car, and I felt so comforted and at peace. I knew in my heart that it was Derek who was intervening on my behalf.

Another interesting thing happened that made it clear to me that Derek was with me and was communicating with me. About a week before I got my new car I was driving to work one morning. It was a beautiful morning, and the sun had just come up creating a gorgeous glow in the sky with gently floating clouds. My old car was producing its typical noises of struggle and strain. Then without my assistance, my windshield wipers went back and forth one single time and then stopped. Now mind you my windshield wipers hadn't worked for a very long time because the motor had completely burned out. So it was impossible for them to be working at this moment. And it never happened again. I knew in my heart it was Derek letting me know he was close. I could hear him saying "Hey mom, it's me! I'm so happy for you that you are going to be getting a new car where your windshield wipers will finally work, and you don't have to be in this piece of junk anymore!"

Besides these events, I have also had two very powerful dreams where I was visited by Derek. In one of the dreams, he comes to me, and we just hug each other for a very long time and tell each other how much we love and miss each other. When I woke up, I felt the most incredible feeling of comfort, love and peace. It was the most intense feeling, and I knew that it was more than just a dream and that he had truly visited me and wanted to tell me that.

In the second dream, Derek is wearing the hat he always used to wear and is smiling and happy. I said to him "You look good!" We both just looked at each other, and there was a feeling of knowingness between us. It felt real, and I knew it was his way of telling me that he was still with me and that wherever he was he was feeling happy and at peace.

All of these things, the blessings that he brought me and the visitations in my dreams allowed me to know without a doubt that Derek is still with me and that we are still connected. More than just the events, it was the feeling of knowingness that it brought me. The tremendous sense of comfort, peace and happiness and it helped me to feel that I can carry on knowing that he has never left my side and is playing a role in bringing good things into my life.

Nana Still Loves Christmas

When I was a young girl, my beloved Nana passed away from a very rare cancer. Nana was the matriarch of the entire family. Everyone flocked to Nana and Grandpa's house for holidays, with Christmas being her favorite. It was a very special time for our whole family. Aunts, uncles, cousins, everyone wanted to be at Nana's house. There was always a special spirit in the air, and the room filled with colored sparkling lights both inside and out with red, green and gold. Special decorations in the front yard including big fat snowmen and Rudolph with a twinkling red nose. Upon entering the house you were immediately greeted warmly by Nana and given something warm to drink, usually some eggnog spiced with rum or some hot apple cider. The smell of spices and turkey bubbling away in the oven would meet you before you even got to the front door. Everyone was welcome, and those who had nowhere else to go for the holidays were always brought into her fold.

When Nana passed away, we were all at a loss as to how to celebrate Christmas in her absence. The tradition lacked the energy and spirit now that Nana was gone.

She was the one who got everyone excited and was the glue that held us all together. Much discussion ensued as to what we were now going to do with the Christmas holiday. What traditions we would keep and which traditions no longer seemed important to continue doing. I think more than anything we were stuck in a place of loss and grief and the sadness sucked the energy out of the holiday. We all just missed Nana. But after much discussion we decided to stay true to Nana's celebration of Christmas and keep all the traditions.

Six months after Nana passed away, our family moved into their house to take care of Grandpa. Of course Grandpa was devastated after losing his beloved wife of forty years. They were high school sweethearts and neither had ever been with anyone else. I think it's hard for us to conceive of such a long loving relationship in these days where people and relationships seem easily disposable. But they were bonded for life and without Nana, Grandpa was depressed and could hardly take care of himself.

My sister and I moved into Nana's old bedroom and neither of us minded or were disturbed by this. We just accepted it as the regular course of things and in a way I was comforted by being in the same room where she had slept. I remember going into her room when we would stay with her and putting my face against her soft and delicate cheek and saying "Nana, wake up, I'm hungry."

Her cheek contained the smell of all of her- the smell was distinctly Nana and was deeply comforting. Her room carried this same smell and it felt like home.

However, the room that I was always afraid of, was the attic and it could only be accessed from Nana's room where we were now staying. The first Christmas since her passing, we were all decorating the house as Nana had done and my Dad was outside stringing the Christmas lights. He had run out, and wanted me to go up into the attic to get more. I was as terrified as ever to go up there, but my dad was the kind of man that you simply did not say no to, and he insisted I go.

As I neared Nana's bedroom, my heart was pounding. I felt as though I could see my chest rising and falling and could hear my heart pounding in my ears. As I climbed the stairs, I was praying that I would be okay and that nothing would be there. I was trying to find the lights as quickly as I could, tearing through boxes and throwing stuff everywhere. In between the tremendous noise I was making in my excited state I heard a scratching noise that sounded like a rodent. As I turned to see what it was, there was Nana standing there looking straight at me! Before I could even think I was already halfway down the attic stairs and then down the other set of stairs heading outside, screaming to my dad. Annoyed because he could see that I didn't have the lights, he asked me what the hell happened. I said, "The

Christmas lights are up in the attic with Nana." He thought I was either playing a joke on him or had lost my mind.

Frustrated at my silly game he stormed up to the attic to get the lights himself. As he came down the attic stairs his mouth was open, his skin was pale and his eyes wide with amazement. Yes, he had seen Nana too. When my dad told my mom and aunt, they went up to the attic too, but they did not see her. Since that unforgettable Christmas day I have seen, spoken to and experienced many signs from loved ones that have passed on. I feel blessed that I saw Nana with my own eyes, as I will never doubt that she is with me and that our loved ones are always with us even though they are on the other side. Though Nana is gone, I know that she is with us, the tradition is alive and that she still loves Christmas.

A Playful Reminder

Kate's mother worked as a wardrobe supervisor at the playhouse for as long as she could remember. One of her favorite things to do as a little child was to go to work with her and play with all the different costumes and props in the wardrobe room. She would hide amongst the long velvet dresses and put on top hats that were so big they covered her entire face. As she got older, she grew to respect and really admire what her mother did. Her mother loved the theater and enjoyed being a part of bringing stories to life. She was a very creative woman and was also a skilled seamstress herself.

When she passed away, it only seemed natural and appropriate to honor this major part of her life in some way. Her family had many discussions to figure out what would be the best way to symbolize her love and passion for the theater. When they ultimately decided to put the "tragedy & comedy" (sad & happy) theater masks on her gravestone, it seemed like the perfect choice. When the family would visit her at the cemetery, it was always comforting to be reminded of the joy that filled her life.

As time passed, the space that Kate's mother left in her life by her absence only seemed to grow bigger. She longed to hear her voice, see her face and feel her arms around her. She wished she could do the simple things with her again: sit out on the porch and talk, share a meal or wander around at fabric stores. More than anything she just wanted a sign that she was still in her life and wasn't gone forever.

Finally one day Kate received the answer to her prayers and the sign she had been continuously asking for. Kate had just arrived at her work's parking lot and was running late. She rushed out of her car and slammed the door shut. As she started to move to the building she kicked a small box that went bumping on the asphalt like a stone skimming the surface of a lake. This caught her attention. The box was brightly colored and decorated with a small rhinestone. It was a beautiful jewelry box. Curious, she reached down to open it and see what was inside. It was a necklace that had a unique charm on it- two masked faces. The same as her mother's gravestone! For a moment, Kate couldn't believe her eyes. The sign was unmistakable. An incredible feeling of comfort, peace and love came over her, and she finally knew that her mother was with her. Her mother had truly sent her a playful reminder, and what a fitting choice it was.

Let It Go

It was a cloudy, cold and overcast day when I got the call that my grandmother had passed away. My husband, a soldier, and I were 2,500 miles away and were stationed in another country. We had been gone for quite a while and even though my grandmother and I would talk on the phone, I felt so distant from her. I felt terrible that we were so far away and longed to be by her side. My grandmother and I were extremely close as I was her only granddaughter. My mother told me that from the time I was born my grandmother had felt a special connection to me.

To be honest, I think my mom may have even been a little jealous that she didn't receive that much attention from her mother. But there is always a special bond between grandparents and their grandchildren and they often lavish the love that they didn't give to their children. I remember my grandmother making me all my favorite foods, teaching me how to sew and having an amazing collection of costume jewelry for me to play with. My grandmother was like a mother to me.

All these memories came like a torrential rain into my mind as my eyes welled with tears upon hearing this terrible news. And the worst part for me was that I learned that my grandma died as a result of the negligence of her nurse. She had prematurely died due to the wrongdoing of another person, and I felt angry and bitter which was unusual for me, being an even minded Libra.

A couple days later my husband and I were looking on the internet trying to figure out the best way to get home for her funeral when a blank page without any URL popped up on our screen. The page was blank white except for the words "I'm still alive". We both sat there looking at the screen, eyes wide in absolute shock and amazement. I looked at my husband's face, and he was as white as the computer screen. We took a screenshot of the page as evidence to prove to ourselves and other people that we weren't going crazy. We both just sat there shaking our heads wondering how this could be and how could she be communicating with us, as she had passed away days ago.

The next few days I couldn't breathe, and I felt so angry. I kept asking in my mind, "Why would that message be there? Why would someone intentionally kill my sweet grandmother?" I kept role playing in my head and imagining those last days and moments of my grandmother's life and how wrong it was. A serious injustice had been done, and the nurse seemed to have suffered no consequence. Out in my backyard, I looked at the mountains off in the distance to try to calm my mind by looking at something beautiful and gain some perspective. I found myself crying and couldn't stop, all these questions spinning in my mind.

Then all of a sudden a little bird flew down in front of me and landed directly in my path. It wasn't scared at all, it just stared directly up at me. An enormous wave of peace came over me and I immediately felt something touch my shoulder so gently, although it made me jump. Of course, I thought someone was behind me, so I quickly turned around to look. Then I heard my grandmother's voice say, "It's me! I'm here! I'm alive. Let it go". Then the bird flew off and I couldn't feel her presence around me anymore.

I was so thrown by what had just happened that my legs felt weak and I quickly dropped to the ground. I sat there hugging my knees into me rocking from side to side trying to process everything that had just happened. Then I finally realized what she was attempting to communicate to me. She was telling me that her spirit is alive and just her vessel is gone. She's not in pain anymore and is no longer suffering. She wanted me to know that the woman that killed her would have to carry that guilt and receive the karma that goes along with her actions. There was nothing for me to do and for me to be upset and angry was only going to harm me. I felt deeply that my grandmother didn't want the way in which she died, to harden my sweet loving spirit.

Before this event I had felt that I was a spiritual person and believed in metaphysical things, but what happened changed my life. I feel that I am open to so much more spiritually because I experienced my grandmother visiting me from the other side in a way that was clear and undeniable. There will never be a shadow of doubt in my mind that she is with me and that all our deceased loved ones are with us. I am so grateful for this experience and this knowledge. I have let the anger go and only gratitude has taken its place. This was the greatest gift my grandmother could have given to me.

Getting Ready To Print

Late spring of 2006, I received a call from my dad. Somehow in my gut I had always known I would receive this call, so in a sense it only felt as though time was catching up with me and us. My dad hadn't taken good care of himself in the last three or four years, and I knew it would just be a matter of time before I found out that he had had a heart attack or some other sudden and tragic health crisis. He had told me in the weeks leading up to this call that he had been feeling particularly unwell and wasn't sure what was going on. I kept encouraging him to go to the doctor, but he was often stubborn to take care of himself.

So it seemed to be a fated call that day when he told me that he was diagnosed with Stage IV stomach cancer. It was very advanced, and it was doubtful as to what treatments would be helpful at that point. Even chemo and radiation seemed like a coin toss. This was particularly hard news for a man like my dad who vacillated between being an atheist and an agnostic his whole life. My dad was a rational person and the idea of God or a higher power simply didn't make sense, and there wasn't enough evidence for it. Having been an attorney for over 45 years, it wasn't easy to make a good case for God. I think as he got older and wondered at the meaning of his life he wanted to feel a greater spiritual connection and tried to meditate on a regular basis. But I think it was seen more in the framework that meditation was scientifically proven to have certain benefits to one's physical and mental health than as a spiritual practice.

So without any faith or belief or even a concept of the afterlife, my dad was suddenly thrown into the gaping hole of darkness that is death, an inevitable ending that is as final as it gets. My dad told my brother, when they were on their way to get a second opinion from another doctor, that he thought that dying was like turning off a light switch. It was just lights out, and that was it. With no hope in sight, my dad sunk into a deep depression that was a letting go of life. Like someone who holds on to the edge of a cliff with a single finger, he just finally gave up. There was nothing to live for and living with the knowledge that the very END was near was too much truth to live with.

As it turned out it was only two short weeks from the time he was diagnosed until the day that he passed away. I was left feeling blindsided- it happened way too fast. It was too much to absorb, and I felt like I was in shock. It was hard to cry even or access the grief around it. There seemed to be an internal disconnection, and I couldn't even reach my own feelings through the magnitude and finality of what had just happened. I attended the memorial and went back home to try to piece it all together with the help of a therapist.

A couple weeks after the memorial I was hanging out in my apartment one night and making my bed. My bedroom faced the backyard, and I had a motion detector light. As motion detector lights do, it went on when something triggered it. I looked around, and there wasn't anything outside. But more than that, the light stayed on and didn't turn off. I thought this very odd and immediately my thoughts went to my dad and I felt his presence with me.

Then a few minutes later my printer turned on and made the sound it makes when it is preparing to print something. The weird thing was that my computer wasn't on, and the printer isn't activated when the computer is off. I thought this was very odd and couldn't figure it out. Then about five minutes later it did the same thing, and the motion detector light remained on this entire time.

While all of this was happening my dad was at the forefront of my mind. I knew that he was causing these things to happen. There is no rational way to explain this, but it was instinct and a knowing. What's interesting is that what's more important than the actual details of what happened (which could easily be explained away), was that I knew there was something significant about it. It wasn't just an electrical oddity, it was an outer manifestation of his presence. I knew that. If there wasn't something significant about it I wouldn't still be thinking of it all these years later and knowing in my being that my dad was with me that night and trying to let me know that he was with me.

I miss him terribly and think of him often. The way that his entire belly shook when he laughed, how he would get red in the face and the skin on his forehead would peel back when he would smile or laugh, his silly jokes, his love of food and cooking and the bear hugs he would give me that would fill me with so much love and comfort that nothing will ever compare to that feeling. But I am comforted in knowing that I did feel him that night, and I can only derive from that that he is also still with me today.

The Lilac Bush

For over 17 years, my lilac bush was bare of flowers. It took death to bring life to my lilac bush and with it the blessing and comfort of knowing that my sister who had passed was still very much with me.

I bought the lilac bush with much hope and visions of gorgeous cone-shaped flowers, their delicate purple petals bursting with fragrance in the springtime. I planted it in April, the crisp morning air gradually taking on the warmth of the afternoon sun as I planted the tree into the front yard so I could see it from my living room window.

Year after year passed, taking me through many life's changes, and yet the lilac bush remained the same through every changing season. My hope of a full and lush purple jewel of a bush had yet to bare a single flower, and I wondered what I had done wrong. Was the soil not nourishing enough? The air too dry and cold? Should I be feeding it fertilizer? I never considered myself a green thumb, so I wasn't surprised. But it certainly didn't seem right that after 17 years there wouldn't be a single bloom. I suppose in a way, I had given up on it.

In 2006, my beautiful, loving sister passed away. It was a devastating event in my life, and the blow of the loss was tremendous. It left a gaping hole in my life that seemed to descend into the center of the earth, black, dark and empty of anything. Almost like a vacuum or a black hole that sucks all life and matter into it. I descended with it into grief that felt like chaos and without end.

Before my sister died, she told us that when she got to the other side she would let us know that she was alright. I missed her terribly and craved this so badly. I wanted to know that not only was she okay, but that she was still present in my life. I needed to know that she didn't vanish into nothingness. I had no idea how this message would come, but I was eagerly awaiting some clear sign where I would know in my heart that it was her.

Several months later, as I went out to get my mail that stood at the edge of the house on the country road, I passed the lilac bush and noticed a purple bud forming on a branch at the bottom of the tree. I almost didn't see it, but I caught the flash of color at the edge of my eye as I passed by. The mail I was carrying dropped out of my hand in a shower of envelopes. I couldn't believe it! My heart fluttered quickly, and I felt a flush of warmth rush into my face. I knew without a doubt in not only my heart but the deepest part of my being that it was my sister letting me know that she was alright and that she was still with me. A comfort engulfed me, and I instantly felt grounded and at peace.

A little while after that initial bloom my younger sister Linda was going through a health crisis and was very depressed. Our entire family felt at a real loss as to what to do to help her. The doctors were doing all that they could, and she was getting the treatment that she needed, but the progress was very slow. Feeling out of control and helpless I went out to the lilac bush and sat down on the damp grass underneath the tree and sincerely prayed to my sister who had passed to put another bloom on the lilac bush to cheer up our sister and to let us know she was there with us.

It wasn't long after I had prayed under the tree that I saw another bloom coming in on the tree. I felt elated! I quickly went into the house and told my sister what had happened and that I had prayed to our sister to put another bloom on the tree to let us know she was there. We all felt a boost of energy, encouragement and comfort.

By this time, I was starting to have fun with this process! It was almost like a game that my sister and I were playing with each other, and I felt an interaction between the two of us in the same way as when she was alive. Throughout the entire year of 2014 I would walk through the garden and admire the lilac bush and talk with my sister. The tree became a symbol of our current bond, and it made me happy to sit by it and watch it through the big window in my living room as I sat on the couch.

I would pray to her, "Put three blooms on the lilac bush" and then in a way that seemed like a unique challenge to her I said "Put four blooms on the lilac bush!" While I was feeling more confident in her presence, to be honest, there was still a part of me that wanted that "extra" bit of confirmation, just a little bit more. And it was also feeling like a fun game that was going on just between her and me.

And wouldn't you know, in the spring of that year there were four blooms on the lilac bush! I stood by the tree looking in amazement and felt an incredible feeling of warmth, love and peace wash over me like a soothing wave. Finally, I knew without a doubt that my sister was with me. I didn't question anymore, and it transformed the grief from a feeling of a dark empty hole to something bittersweet.

I took a picture of the four blooms for my sister Linda, as I had been telling her the story all along of how I would go to the lilac bush and pray to our sister for lilac flowers on our tree. She was always deeply comforted by this in the same way I was, and it helped her tremendously. Her energy immediately picked up after the first flowering and her condition continued to improve.

Throughout the years, we have both have similar "visitations" from our sister, and yet the lilac bush remains a symbol that love never dies and in fact, it can bring new life.

Thank You Mum

December was just around the corner, and I thought as I stirred a pot of spaghetti for my dinner. The holidays were a special time for me as my two grown children and my grandchildren usually came over for an extended visit. My mind was on the preparations I would need to make in the next few weeks.

I checked to see if the food was ready and then something happened that I had no rational explanation for. My left arm lifted itself and came to rest over my right breast. Immediately, I felt the hard lump underneath. My mouth went dry and my mind refused to focus but one thought swum in my mind. My mum had done it. She had lifted my arm and placed it over my breast knowing that it was the only way to get through to me.

You see, mum had passed on from breast cancer. She had been diagnosed with it when she was sixty-one years old and had fought it for the next twenty years. It had returned three times until it finally got her when she was eighty-one. Her family had had a history of cancer and it was highly likely that I would get it too. She had tried to tell me this on the last months when she could still talk.

I would interrupt her and tell her that everything would be alright. I saw the impatience in her eyes when I wouldn't discuss the subject of breast cancer but I couldn't handle it. Mum was a planner all her life and she liked to talk everything under the sun while I, on the other hand, preferred to keep away from painful subjects.

She knew this about me and soon gave up but each time I looked into her eyes, I could see the worry that like her a daughter, I would get the disease in the future. She read pamphlets and pushed them into my hand and I told her that I would read them at home. I never did.

My way of coping over the years after mum's death was denial. I never gave it a thought and neither did I pay attention to the information on TV and in newspapers informing people about cancer and screening. I went about my life, studiously ignoring the fact that I was at high risk of contracting the disease.

Mum and I had been exceptionally close, being just the two of us in our family. My dad had passed on years earlier when I was six years old. Mum was a talkative person and quite aggressive, unlike myself who had dad's personality, as mum said. She had achieved so much by the time of her death.

We talked about everything from the problems I had as I grew up to her hopes for me for the future. Seeing her sick was heartbreaking, more so in the last year before she passed on. She spent the last six months in a hospice near my home where I could be with her every day. Mum faced her illness with courage, even when the doctors finally told her that her body was not strong enough to undergo any more procedures.

At first she appeared to be bouncing back and would chat as much as she used to and then without warning, she started to change. Her memory would fail her and it broke my heart when she called me by her sister's name. The last few weeks of her life were painful to watch. Despite pain medication, she moaned and twisted in her bed and her breath came out in loud gasps, as though she was struggling to breathe.

As much as I wanted mum to live, I was grateful when she finally passed away and was at peace. No more pain I told myself but that did not erase the memories of her suffering. Her mother, my grandmother, had also died of breast cancer but I was a child then and never saw her suffering. But with mum, I was there all the way and on some nights after the funeral, I would wake up sweating, remembering her anguished cries and calls for me to end the pain.

Over time, I slowly go over my grief but not over my fear of cancer. If I didn't' think of it, I would not get it, I told myself and I did just that. I worked, attended to my small garden over the weekends or a social gathering in the community where I lived.

I was sixty-one when my mum took my hand and placed it on my breast. I could deny what I didn't know but once I felt the lump, I was confronted by reality. I couldn't sleep that night and I touched the lump throughout the evening, unable to believe that all along it had been there, steadily growing.

In the middle of the night, I got up from the bed and went to the living room and switched on the TV. The first thing I saw was an announcement and a free cancer screening. I jotted down the 800 number and the following morning I called and made an appointment. It was cancer and the doctors said that I was lucky I had caught it so early. It was stage one.

I had a lumpectomy and over the next six months, underwent chemo and radiation. I can only credit the courage I faced the illness with, to my mum. I believe that from beyond, mum had infused me with her special brand of bravery because I never once wept or fell into depression.

That was six years ago. My heart swells with gratitude to my mum, for lifting my hand and placing it on the lump in my breast. I was given a clean bill of health and all that is because of mum. She was a mother even after passing on, look after my health and ensuring that I got the help that I needed. Thank you, mum.

Wheel Of Fortune

I have been a nurse in a long term care facility for many years. I have witnessed the stages in the process of death many times. It has become a familiar and almost predictable process to me. I have seen many interesting things occur that reflects there is life after death and that indeed death is not an ending. I feel grateful that I have seen this with my own eyes and have seen it play out in many different ways. But for me, my story is the most interesting and most dear to my heart. And it came at a time when my sisters and I needed it most.

It was 2002 and my older sisters and I were surrounding my mother in her bed at the hospice center. We all knew that her passing was imminent. We sat there in our chairs, looking at each other, at my mother and being absorbed in our inner world of emotions and reflection. It seemed surreal that this moment had come, and yet it also seemed a natural, predictable progression of events that we had become adapted to. My mother looked so weak, and I didn't want her to struggle or be uncomfortable anymore.

Then the moment came that I knew signaled the end. After not opening her eyes for days my mother suddenly opened her eyes wide, turned her head and stared intently at something over my shoulder. The expression on her face was both a look of surprise and happiness. She let out a breath and passed away. I felt a breath go out of my sisters and me as well. The room seemed to take on the heaviness of this monumental moment that marked the end of the presence of our mother in our lives.

We lingered around the hospice for a little while, handling all of the mundane details that occur when a life ends, and in a surrendered fog caravanned to my mother's condo. It was late afternoon at this point and dusk was approaching. The sky was taking on a pinkish golden hue, and horizontal streaks of clouds dotted the landscape. As we entered her condo, it felt strange to be there without her and also with the knowledge that she wouldn't be coming back. Her things seemed to take on an empty quality without her there. As if they had no purpose.

Mom's condo was a one bedroom with a small lounge you entered into, and then a tiny kitchen off to the left. You couldn't swing a cat in there. After taking everything in for a few moments, we set to work going through her paperwork and shredding old financial documents trying to get things in order.

We were like an assembly line of workers, my oldest sister sitting stretched out on the couch with her feet up reading papers while my other sister was sitting shredding the documents. I had taken a break from my duties on "the line" and had escaped to my mother's room seeking comfort and closeness to her. I took some time touching and smelling everything, trying to inhale as much of her essence as I could carry with me. As I was leaving her room and began walking down the hallway, the ancient TV in the lounge suddenly turned on by itself, and the television audience called out "Wheel of Fortune."

All of us jumped as though we had been shocked with electricity and we checked to see if someone had accidentally sat on the remote and turned on the TV. We searched and searched everywhere until finally we found the remote on the kitchen counter where none of us had been and turned the TV off. Now mind you this is an old TV with an even more elderly owner and no cable. My mom didn't have the right technology nor the ability to set up a TV on a primer, and she had been out of her condo for two weeks before her death.

My sisters and I stayed there while we held vigil for our mom, and the TV never turned on by itself again. The best part of this whole experience was that "Wheel of Fortune" was my mom's favorite show! She never missed it, and we all knew never to call mom when it was "Wheel of Fortune" time. My sisters and I just sat there looking at each other feeling the full impact of what had just happened and then all at once started laughing. Then in unison we said, "Mom always told us to call when we made it where we were going so she would know that we were safe. She's calling to tell us she made it home". We had all experienced something that we will always treasure as being positive assurance that our mother was okay and that she was still with us. I am so grateful for this, and I am also happy to know that even in the afterlife my mother didn't lose her sense of humor!

No Time Limit

I had heard that people would sometimes be visited by their loved ones in their dreams, and I always wondered if that happened, and if so was it more than a dream? Well, today I had my answer, and I now know from my experience that it most definitely is more than a dream, and it is the most beautiful refreshing experience that one could ever hope to have.

Last night I had the most incredible dream of my grandmother and when I woke up today I was sobbing rivers of tears. It's an hour later, and I am still crying. The dream started in my mother's house where my grandmother lived as well. My grandmother passed in 2004, and it remains the most devastating event of my life. So I am in my house, and I am downstairs helping an old friend file away pictures because his friend had passed away. I don't know why it was all happening in my house because I didn't know this girl too well- but she did, in fact, die two years ago. I helped my friend get the pictures together and meanwhile there is a whole crowd of people in my house, some people that I know like family members and some people I don't know at all.

As I look out of the big bay window that is in the living room at the front of my house, I see my grandmother in the yard. She had her back turned towards me and she was talking to some people outside. I hesitated to go outside because I was in shock that I was seeing her. Standing there frozen, I was at a loss as to what to say or do. But then I couldn't wait any longer and the excitement of seeing her took over and I ran outside. I tapped her gently on her shoulder, and she slowly turned around and gave me the biggest smile as she was so happy to see me. Immediately I started crying uncontrollably.

She hugged me so tenderly and lovingly as only a grandmother could and the tears gushed down my face. As I cried more, she hugged me even harder. It seemed so incredibly real and it is hard to put into words. While we were hugging each other, she said to me "I promise I have never forgotten about you. Promise not to forget about me." When she said those words I thought to myself "I have never forgotten about you and never will." I then tried to compose myself a little and said to her "Okay Grandma." I patted her on the back as if to say goodbye, but she knew I was still hurting. I tried to step back, but she wouldn't let me go. With this incredible show of love by my grandmother, I completely lost it again and started sobbing.

I'm not sure what happened right after this, but I do remember walking around the house alone to cry my eyes out in private. The next thing I knew I was waking up and coming out of the dream, still crying. The more I reflected on the dream, the more emotional I would get. I was so moved by the dream because I know it was real. I felt the happiness in the dream and the amazing hug that we had where we both didn't want to let go.

It was so great to see her again after 11 years, hug her and have her tell me that she hasn't forgotten me. To hear her say that she still loves me and that she doesn't want me to forget about her. I am so happy that after such a long time I finally was visited by her. I have missed her so much! I have dreamed about her sometimes but no dream was ever like that. There was a different quality to the dream. It didn't feel like a dream. It felt real. I still wonder why it took so long, but I was happy in the dream just to hug her and cry on her shoulder.

On the other hand, I'm not surprised that she visited me, even if it did take a long time. I had a very special relationship with my grandmother. She wasn't just my grandmother. She watched over me as a child and was the only one who showed me love. I know that my mother loves me, but it's hard for her to communicate that. She would say, "That's just not the type of family we are." But my grandmother was the emotional one and would tell me she loved me a million times a day and took such good care of me too. It was an incredible loss when she passed away, but at least now I have this dream to hold on to and the knowledge that she did come to see me. I will always be comforted by remembering the hug that we had and her soothing words and love. I don't know why it took so long, and I hope it happens again, but I am so grateful I was able to see her at least one more time.

Time To Go

I grew up in a small town in the Midwest. The kind of town where everyone knows each other, and it's not uncommon for a person to be born and die in the same hospital. It's a delightful town with beautiful maple trees lining the streets and where kids can play safely outside. Everything that you need is on the main street in town, and the stores are mostly family owned and run businesses where you can find three generations working under the same roof.

There was a boy that I grew up with that went to the same school, and we had the same circle of friends. Mike was a tall, somewhat lanky boy with chocolate brown eyes that reflected warmth and soul. He had a great sense of humor and a lot of enthusiasm and energy. He played a few different sports and always seemed to be going from one activity to another. He was six years younger than me which is a lot when you are a teenager. In those younger years, that kind of an age gap is like a broad expanse of ocean separating two different continents. We were on entirely different developmental schedules, and I just considered him someone's "little bro." At that time he was on the outskirts of my awareness. He wasn't a peer and certainly wasn't old enough for me to be interested in romantically.

Well, as I said, in a small town you know the goings on of almost everyone. You see people grow older, mature and develop their unique personality that is always changing. When I was around 25 and Mike was 19 we ran into each other at the local coffee shop. We had occasionally seen each other briefly around town, perhaps crossing the street or driving around. But nothing really "registered" on each of our radars. But when we saw each other at the coffee shop something dramatically shifted. So, of course, it seemed to me completely out of the blue when he told me that he loved me and had always felt this way about me. I think my jaw must have dropped open because I had no idea.

When he shared this with me, everything changed. Of course, it was hard for me to trust him and fully give myself to the relationship at first because I had been burned before and I was concerned that our age difference was too much. But gradually I let my guard down as he made me feel more special and loved than anyone in my life. Unlike the past relationships that I had had where it was all talk and no action, he consistently showed me how much he cared and how devoted he was. It was easy to fall in love with him, and we both fell in love with each other. It was the sweetest, most precious time in my life.

A few months later it was Halloween night and we were both going to separate parties. Before we went out, we spoke on the phone and he told me that he would call me when he got home. I finished my party around midnight and went home to go to sleep. I got in bed and laid there anxious and worried because I hadn't heard from him yet. He was always so good about calling me. I feared something was seriously wrong. This was completely out of character for him. My heart was pounding, my mouth was dry, and I felt as though someone was sitting on my chest. I couldn't even begin to fall asleep.

Around 2 am my phone rang, and I felt both scared and excited. It was Mike's friend, and he told me that Mike had supposedly passed out in the middle of a country road, and a drunk driver had driven over him. I was in shock and devastated. I really couldn't believe his words and that this was happening. It felt like a horrible nightmare. It was simply too much for me to wrap my mind around.

He was in the hospital in a coma and I just couldn't bring myself to see him. It felt too much for me to bear. This was the man that I loved more than any man I had ever met and I just couldn't see him like that. I was in communication with his family and friends and they told me that his situation was dire and it didn't look like he would ever come out of the coma. His injuries were extensive and it appeared he had severe brain damage.

Right before Thanksgiving I had the most vivid, powerful dream I had ever had. I dreamt that he knocked on my door and gave me a hug and kiss and told me that he couldn't handle being in the hospital anymore. He said that he knew that he would never be normal again, so he left. This was more than a dream; it felt like a real visitation.

The next day his family called to tell me that he had passed, but I felt like I already knew. I knew that it was him who had come to me the night before and was telling me that he was letting go of this life. Of course, I understood. Being in a coma was no way to live and there was no hope that he would come out of it. I felt loved and reassured that he came to tell me that before he let go. It also made me realize without a doubt that our spirit is not connected to our body and that he is still with me. Nevertheless, my heart has been broken ever since. That was about 35 years ago and I still can't forget. I have never felt the same about anyone ever since. He was the love of my life and I hold on to the thought that he must still be with me because true love never dies.

A Promise Kept

My husband Larry passed away on Feb. 4, 2015. I remember the last moments with him so clearly, as if they were painted in vivid deep strokes and I can feel every detail as it plays out in slow motion. I was sitting with him as he laid motionless on the hospital bed, his energy and life diminishing by the second. This strong man filled with vitality, warmth and love was slipping away from me as I sat helplessly watching, surrendering to the greatest inevitability of Life itself. He was my foundation and my rock, and I held his hand until his last breath. As painful as it was, I saw it as my final duty as his wife to be strong and supportive and be there with him until the end. As his last breath floated quietly out of his mouth, there was a look of peace upon his face.

The day after he passed I walked around in a daze. I felt so disoriented, like I was on drugs or drunk. I felt completely lost and didn't know what to do with myself other than carrying my body from room to room like a ghost. My world seemed like it had ended too and I had arrived at the last page of a novel and I had no idea what would come next. I collapsed at the edge of my bed sobbing inconsolable tears. It was scary to be caught in such overpowering grief and emotion that it seemed it would have no end. My only wish of comfort was to feel held by Larry and to know that he was with me. I cried out to him to hold me. Almost immediately I felt a warmth on my left side. It felt as though a strong light had been focused on my leg and I could feel not only warmth but an actual presence. I hoped that it was him and not my imagination or unstable mental state creating stories.

About two weeks after he died I was sitting in my living room after dinner watching something mindless on the television when the lights in my house started to flicker and then went out for about 25 seconds. When the power came back on, his old clock radio in the basement started playing classical music, lasted about three minutes and then stopped. It was strange because he only listened to rock music, so I was perplexed as to why it would be playing a station that he never had it on. Also, I almost never had any power outage in my house except in extreme weather, and this had been a bright spring day. His clock radio hadn't been touched in months and it just sat down there with the time flashing wit the radio never making a sound.

Another sign that I have received that lets me know that my husband is still with me is that now and then I can smell him. How can one ever begin to explain the distinctive smell of the one that they love? But you know it when you smell it. It's a smell that doesn't just enter your nose; it enters your whole being. It's almost primitive. For example, last week I was taking my small children on the highway to the beach and as I entered my car and opened the door his smell strongly washed over me. I just sat there frozen for a minute in the car, soaking up the smell and feeling of his presence. After a long day at the beach, when I returned to my car I could smell him again. This time, it didn't happen when I opened the door, but rather I noticed it at the end as we approached the house. The most interesting part to me was that both times that this happened it was in my vehicle that I bought six months after his death so there would be no chance of him having been in my new vehicle.

I've also had dreams that he's still sick but alive. These aren't just ordinary dreams but dreams with an entirely different weight and power. I don't just see images; I feel an energy of his presence. I have continued to have episodes where the lights flicker in the house, and they don't always happen in the same spot. One time it happened in my bedroom as I was reading a book. Another time it happened in the kitchen when I was cooking dinner. Each time it completely took me by surprise, and I felt it was Larry letting me know that he was still sharing my everyday routine with me.

I think that what touches me the most about all these signs that I have received is that when he was close to death I asked him if he could give me signs when he died that he was still with me. I remember him looking at me with a twinkle in his eye and saying "I'll see what I can do." When I had asked him that, I knew that I would be feeling lonely and would need to feel that reassurance that his spirit was still alive and to feel his presence in my life. I feel like he kept his promise to me and continues to let me know that he is still in my life. I miss him so much, but the signs that he has given me has helped me tremendously through this difficult time.

Thumbs Up

John was my older brother by ten years and I looked up to him from when we were growing up until I was eighteen. He lost his life on my eighteenth birthday, as he was coming home from his job as a mechanic. John never went to college but he was determined that I would. He and mum put away money every month so that by the time I got to eighteen there would be enough money to pay for my tuition fees.

This was an enormous sacrifice on mum and John's part and I could see the toll it was taking on them having to take care of the household expenses as well as save up for me. For John, it was an even bigger sacrifice. In the last five years, he had moved back home so that he could cut down on his expenses. I had also met his girlfriend, a lovely girl by the name of Lora.

John kept a hold on all his plans for the future so that my dream of going to college would be realized. Every evening I prepared dinner and waited for John and mum to get back home. John usually arrived first, his brown hair bouncing as he walked in. I would tease him about the grease on his hands and the sweat clinging to his work clothes.

After a shower, he would join me in the living room, and we would chat as we waited for mum to come home from her job as a sales clerk in a department store. We had a beautiful routine that I loved and looked forward to. The day of my birthday, June 21st was on a Tuesday. I baked my cake and cooked a special dinner for the three of us to share.

John didn't come at his usual time but I wasn't anxious figuring he had dashed to the stores to get my birthday present. I even chuckled as I visualized him running from store to store and agonizing over what to get me. He tended to do things at the last minute and his lateness did not bother me, even when mum came home.

An hour later, the worry kicked in. Darkness had set in and still John had not come. Just then, we got the phone call that would turn our world upside down. John had had an accident and died on the spot. The next days were a blur for me and I have no idea how I managed to get through his funeral.

The sun shone and people went about their lives while mum and I seemed stuck in a rut of grief. She put on a cheerful face but I saw the new worry lines that had come on her face. Mum dealt with her grief by going over John's things in his room, while I couldn't stand any reminders of my brother.

She made a small shrine for him in the living room, over the mantel. Pictures of a laughing John, his hats, favorite colognes and anything she could find that reminded her of him. His ashes were the centerpiece of this arrangement. While I understood mum's need to do this, I never associated the mementoes on the wall with the caring and loving brother I had known.

I wanted to get a nursing degree as I wanted to help people but the burning ambition I had, was gone. I couldn't seem to summon up the strength to fill the forms needed to confirm my place in college. Time moved and yet I did nothing. Mum was too wrapped up in her grief and survival to notice that I had not sent off the forms. She sometimes had to work thirty-six-hour shifts just to make ends meet. Without John's input, things were even tougher for her but she soldiered on and never gave up.

Two weeks after John's funeral, I sat in the living room looking at the shrine mum had created. For some reason this particular day, it struck a chord with me and my heart ached for John. Mum got home after one of her long shifts and I went to the kitchen to greet her. John had always made a fuss of her when she got home after long hours of work, greeting her happily and welcoming her home.

Her eyes were red and I could tell that she had been crying on the way home. I gave her a hug, and then this loud bang sounded from the living room. We both rushed there to see what had caused it. The flowers and the pictures of John from the shrine that mum had made had crashed to the floor. There was no wind or anything I could see that would have caused them to fall.

That was not all. Right in the middle of the flowers and the pictures was one eight by ten framed picture of John. It lay right in the center of the rest. It fell face up and he appeared to be smiling straight at us. What struck mum and I was the position of the picture. Being the closest to the edge of the mantel, the picture should have fallen face down, rather than facing up.

We held hands and looked at it in awe. At that moment, we both knew that it was John's way of reaching out to us and especially to mum to welcome her back after a long day and night at work. Needless to say, I filled the forms and sent them off. We both needed to know that John's soul had not died but had lived on. It was comforting to know that he was watching us from beyond as he had when he was alive. When I got my degree, I held it up into the air and grinned, knowing that John was smiling back at me and giving me a thumbs up.

Mixed Messages

I have had many different types of messages and visitations from the other side, so my experience has been that the ways in which loved ones communicate with us are as varied and unique as they are. For example, my father would come to me in my dreams and from the things he would say it appeared that he had moved on to a new life on the other side. I could feel his presence strongly with me, so I knew it was more than a dream. But it also felt like my father was creating a new life and wanted to get permission from us and share his new experiences. He would always look younger and very healthy. Once he came to my mother asking her permission to marry. Another time he visited my sister saying he was going to be a father. Then he came to me telling me he was moving and looking for new furniture. He passed over 28 years ago.

Another experience that I had been with a friend who died two years ago and his primary way of communicating with me was through sound and vibration. Not long after his passing, every morning my bedroom door would rattle. Of course, this had never happened before, and there was no apparent reason for it.

At first it didn't occur to me to think that it might be him as I didn't make the connection between those two things. But then one morning out of the blue I had this flash of insight, and I realized that he was trying to communicate with me.

Once I realized that it was him, I would start talking to him. If he rattled the door too early in the morning and woke me up, I would say to him, "I'm sleeping, come back later!" The rattle would stop immediately and then start again when I had awoken. When I would put my hand on the door, I could feel the door shaking. This would go on for about a year until I decided to share it with my mother. My mom has experienced visitations from many loved ones throughout her life, and she suggest I tell him gently and lovingly to move on. She said that often they need to be encouraged to move on because they get stuck in the comfort and familiarity of this plane of existence.

Probably my most impressive experience of visitation was with my best friend who passed away about 16 months ago. He left behind two lovely daughters in their 20's. I hear his voice in my head all the time, and he comes through music and many unusually colored pigeons. He raised pigeons almost his entire life. Recently I saw a white spotted bird, and I knew it was a sign from him.

Recently his daughter was getting married, and I went shopping to find a particular gift for her. I walked into a ceramic shop, and I could hear his voice saying clearly and emphatically, "What about me? I need to get them a gift too". I couldn't believe it, as a moment later I looked up and saw a clock with musical notations on it. I could hear the enthusiasm in his voice as he told me that he wanted that to be his gift to them. He had been a keyboard player and musician and music was an essential part of who he was and how he lived his life.

When I wrapped the gift and placed in the envelope reading "Open this first". The note card had a detailed description of the story of how her father handpicked her wedding gift for her. Upon reading that card, she burst into tears and told me that the gift was perfect. She knew immediately that the gift was from her dad. I don't think she could have received a more special gift. Both she and her sister know that I was very close to their father, and I think they see me as a sort of messenger from him. When he first died, he would contact me all the time to check on them to make sure that his wishes were being carried out. It was sweet to see a father checking lovingly on his daughters from the other side. It has truly been an amazing and touching experience.

I am now taking a class on Indigenous Chicanos although I am not a Chicano, it's just an interesting subject to me. My instructor shared with us one day that many people that have passed on get sort of stuck before they move on. He said he believed it was because they are helping their loved ones deal with the grieving process. I know that in my experience this has been true. It was certainly the case with my friend and his daughters.

It's comforting to know that there is still life on the other side and that our loved ones are still around. All the many different types of messages and visitations I have received has shown me that. My friend was so accepting of death, and now I see that in a way he didn't die at all. While it's comforting to know that this isn't the end when we die, I am aware that I have a lot more living to do. I just hope that I get to it all first!

So Many Signs

I feel incredibly grateful that I have had so many different signs from loved ones who have passed on, especially from my beloved mother. I have experienced hearing messages through many different senses, especially sight, hearing and touch. For example, I once heard her voice very clearly. It felt like I was both hearing her with my ears, but at the same time it had a quality that you hear on EVP recordings too. Another time soon after she had passed I was sitting on the couch reminiscing about old times and happy memories, my mind drifting into space. All of a sudden I felt her very clearly kiss my on the cheek. This was not the air, or a draft-this was a smack dab concentrated kiss. It was like I could feel the weight of it placed on my cheek and the texture of her lips.

One time she put a photo of herself in the middle of the stair landing so that I wouldn't miss it and attempted to appear to me by causing a massive power surge that affected all parts of my house. There was nothing else that would have explained that and it had never happened before. I just knew in my heart that it was her.

I felt like she was pulling out all the stops to get my attention.

The most incredible experience that occurred was when I was having a day at the park taking pictures. Just for fun I was taking multiple photos of the front of my car with my cell phone as I had noticed that the reflection of the clouds in the windshield looked very cool. After I had taken some of them, I scrolled back through them to see how they had turned out. All but one of them were just regular clouds reflected in the windshield. The next picture I saw made me lose my breath- I stood there for a few moments frozen in amazement. In the photo, I saw my mother's likeness exactly- her face and the outline of her head and shoulders as if she was sitting in the passenger seat of my car. What was most remarkable about this was that my mom never drove, and I always drove her around like we were best friends. My mother always sat next to me in the passenger seat like we were two peas in a pod. So it made perfect sense that the reflection of her image would be in the passenger side of my car as this was her spot.

As if this wasn't incredible enough, coming off of that image to the upper right was another image of her, a smaller image where she had a huge smile on her face. The most amazing thing to me was that when I arrived at the park I took a few minutes to meditate and pray to please give me a sign in the clouds. Part of me couldn't believe it! I was overjoyed by the whole experience and so grateful to have an obvious sign of my mother's presence.

My father also sadly left us suddenly last June. When I arrived from out of state to his home where he passed, he would do things like flicker the lights for me. Just today I had another interesting experience. I was thinking of my deceased family as I parked the car at the store and when I opened the door to get out, there were not one, but many pennies strewn on the ground right next to the door. There were only pennies and no other coins. This may not seem like a strange occurrence or a sign from loved ones, but I just knew in my soul that it was a sign from them.

I have had so many signs, and I love getting them. But one of them that I have received feels particularly dear to me. Soon after my mom passed, I had said a sincere request and prayer to please contact her before I laid down to sleep. Seemingly right after I fell asleep, I found myself standing in a bedroom which seemed so real and vivid. Suddenly my mother walked in dressed in a plush velvet purple robe and big Velcro rollers she had always worn in her hair. I was in complete awe and told myself "Please don't let this be some stupid dream." Then my mom did a playful twirl around with arms raised and said "See? Look at me - I am great!" She then said to me "Mama loves you all very much." I chuckled to myself that she referred to herself as "Mama". Then she walked to me and took me in her arms and held me. I truly felt her presence, and her hug felt exactly as it always had when she was alive. There is a way that a mother can hug you that no one else can. That's when my joy overwhelmed me, and I started to cry. Mom said, "Aww, you love your Mama so much." It was exactly the kind of thing that she would say all the time and it sounded exactly like her. She continued holding me for what seemed like an endless time until I woke up and our visit ended.

There have been so many signs from my loved ones, but each one has been very precious to me. I continue to receive signs and messages all the time. It's incredibly comforting to know that my family is still around me, and I am always looking forward to the next creative way they are going to show me!

Holy Mother's Spirit

My mother passed away in 2001, and it was the most crushing thing that had ever happened to me. My mother and I were very close, and she was a constant part of my life so I guess you could say she was my touchstone. No matter what was happening in my life, my mother was a continuous source of support and unconditional love. When she passed away I prayed and prayed that I would see her as I deeply longed to feel her presence again.

One night I was praying before I went to bed as I usually did, praying to see my mother again so that I could tell her how much I missed her and loved her. I prayed myself to sleep and drifted into a very deep sleep. Finally, my prayer was answered. My mother came to me in my dream, however, it did not feel like a dream at all. It was so vivid and so surreal that I will never forget it or its tremendous impact on me.

The dream started out where I was in darkness kneeling down praying the same prayer as I did while I was awake. When I was done praying, I took a few steps and then looked up above my head towards the ceiling. A few feet above my head I saw my mother's face. As she got closer, she had a bright glow around her that looked like the warm glow given off by a candle in the darkness. It was so beautiful and radiant. I must admit that this was all very frightening to me as it was so real and unexpected. This was something beyond my imagination or realm of experience. As I become frightened, her image started to fade away, and I became sad that I would lose her. I turned around and started praying again to God promising that I will not be frightened. I finally built up the courage and turned back around.

From up above, my mother started coming down closer to me. She appeared to be around 30, her hair was a silky, rich black color, and her eyes were like black diamonds, sparkly and deep as the ocean. I had never seen anything so beautiful and it was magical. She had her permanent teeth again (she wore dentures as she got much older). As she approached closer, I could only see her from the waist up. I said "Hi Mom" and she bent her head softly to the side and said hello back. It was her voice, but the tone of her voice was the most beautiful indescribable tone that doesn't even seem to exist here on earth. It had a vibration that was like nothing I had ever experienced- truly otherworldly.

She smiled back, and I felt this incredible feeling as if it was the Holy Spirit that came from within her that hit me like a ton of bricks. I had never felt anything like it.

My mother put her arms around me and gave me the warmest loving hug. I kept repeating over and over again that I loved her more than anything and how much I missed her. Again in her voice but with that most beautiful tone she said "Oh I love you too so very much." That is when I started crying buckets of tears and wouldn't let go because I had never felt so much love, peace and happiness in my entire life. I felt this flow from within her soul into my soul.

Once I stopped crying, I noticed she was suddenly gone. I also noticed that I was no longer in the same spot anymore. It's like she floated me over to a different area and I was now in darkness. As I turned my head to the right, she wasn't there. But I had this strong feeling that someone was looking at me. I turned my head slowly to the left and there she was far away across the room. I could now see her from the waist down, and I could see the glowing warmth of her spirit. As she approached closer to me, my mother started swaying back and forth. When she was a few feet away, the bottom of her spirit appeared raggedy, longer on one end than the other. It swayed back and forth as if there was a fan blowing.

Then she looked over my shoulder and turned her head smiling and looking to her right as if someone was speaking to her. I felt strongly that she was about to leave me. I shook my head with panic and desperately cried "Mom don't go! Please don't go!" She turned and looked at me surprised that I knew she was leaving. She then smiled and said in that heavenly tone, "Oh don't worry. We will be together again soon." Then she suddenly floated above my head. Once again I could only see her face. She tilted her head again to the right and smiled a sweet, comforting smile. Just as before it felt like the Holy Spirit hit me like a ton of bricks. The most incredible love and peace powerfully took over me. I bent my head and smiled back and then quickly she was gone. I will cherish my mother's visit for the rest of my life here on Earth. This was the most incredible blessing one could ever hope to receive, and I will never doubt her presence or that of the Holy Spirit in my life.

Ding Dong

My mother passed away about a year ago, and the most common way that she contacts me is through my door bell. I bought my doorbell quite a few years ago, and I was attracted to the fun upbeat tune that it plays when you ring it. It was more unique than the classic sound and seemed fun to me. The doorbell only plays the one tune, so I must say in retrospect it has gotten a little boring.

However, soon after my mother passed away, occasionally when someone would ring the doorbell it would chime twice - "ding dong"! The weird part? Only my mom could make it ring twice. It's funny because when my mom was alive she and I would joke about my doorbell ring and she would tease me and say "Why can't you just have a regular doorbell ring like everyone else?! It's only a doorbell!" I had always been the type of person to do things differently and in my way.

Once my husband had the chimes down off the wall as it needed to have the batteries changed. He had to go to the hardware store to buy new ones. While he was at the shop I was taking care of some things around the house when I heard a "ding dong". I couldn't believe it and I stood dead in my tracks. She rang it twice as it lay there on the counter just to show us she could! This was absolute proof to me that my mother was around. There was simply no explaining this.

Many times it has happened that she rings as my daughter either calls on the phone or walks in the door. My daughter and my mother were very close, and it is of no surprise to me that she wants her to know that her grandmother is with her. When I was working a lot, my mother would be the one that would take care of her after school, and they would hang out and do her homework together.

I've also noticed that when the doorbell chimes my dogs bark like crazy but when mom rings they don't bark at all. This has happened so many times that there is no doubt in my mind that there is a pattern here. When my mom rings, they just lay there and are completely relaxed and motionless.

I had another devastating loss in my family recently- this time it was my child. My 36-year-old son was killed in a motorcycle accident on the 18th of March this year. Not long after his passing, my doorbell rang three times "ding ding ding". It had never rang three times before and I feel confident that it was him letting me know he was with me. For some reason, my doorbell has become a channel through which my loved ones visit me and let me know of their presence. There is something humorous about the whole thing, but then again my family always did have a good sense of humor.

The Kid Whisperer

A friend of mine, "Robert" passed away January 14, 2015, from suspected overdose and suicide. I knew my friend had been struggling with life and had episodes of deep depression, but it was still a shock to all of us when it happened. In the days that followed, I cried only once since the day I found out that he had passed away. It disturbed me that I wasn't able to cry more about his death. It felt as though my emotions were frozen in ice and I was numb. I struggled with getting my emotions to thaw out and flow through me, but part of me just wasn't able to come to terms with the fact that he was gone. It all seemed so surreal.

In the past, whenever someone close to me has died, I would have a vivid dream where they would come and say goodbye and let me know they are okay. This has happened to me many times, and I become comfortable with this as some sort of routine after someone has passed away. The way it feels when they visit me in the dream is the same as what other people have described in articles that I have read. There is more clarity and lucidity in the dream and it doesn't feel like I am lost in a dream world. It feels like it is happening in reality and

I am seeing them with waking eyes. Their body appears to have substance, and it seems like I could reach out and touch the person. When I wake up, I need to take a few moments to take it all in. There is something that feels powerful about it and has a strong impact on me. A couple times I have also awoken in tears begging them for just a second or two more so that I can give them one more hug before they go. It feels as though I am always longing for more because it seems so real.

The only times that I have noticed a deviation in my receiving messages from loved ones from the other side is when they have taken their life. This happened with "Robert" and another friend awhile back. With this previous friend who also died from suicide, it took two long years before I finally got to say goodbye. I'm starting to wonder if committing suicide creates some sort of a delay or a barrier to being able to communicate messages to the other side.

However, I did receive a message from "Robert" who passed recently but it was delivered by other means. My nine-year-old son. My son, like many in our family, is very much in tune with spirit. My son had only met "Robert" once, and it was a few weeks before his passing. But afterward my son told me how awesome he thought this fellow was.

Earlier tonight, after arriving home from a visit to our local Fall Fair, my son randomly said to my husband "Daddy, you know what made Mummy really sad? When her friend 'Robert' killed himself. It's ok to cry, Mummy. 'Robert' wouldn't want you to be sad forever."

I immediately got chills running throughout my body, and I got goosebumps on my arms. I never told my son how "Robert" had died, just that he had gone to heaven. At nine, I didn't feel my son was old enough to know the truth yet. Suicide is a complicated thing to explain to a child and could lead to questions that would leave him feeling disturbed and troubled. It simply didn't seem like relevant information to him. So I only mentioned it briefly and never spoke of it again in his presence. So there was absolutely no way he could have known that "Robert" had committed suicide.

As I reflect back on the course of events, I truly feel as though "Robert" wanted to get a message to me but for some reason couldn't do it the traditional way that I'm accustomed to. So instead he used my son as the channel through which to communicate the message. I feel touched that my friend visited me in his unique way, and it's comforting to know that he is okay. It also speaks volumes to me because "Robert" was fantastic with kids. He was what you could call a "Kid Whisperer." Children adored him immediately and felt good being around him. So it's no surprise that my son was a natural choice to receive his message. I'm sure he enjoyed hearing from him.

Many Deaths,
Many Visitations

Most people can't conceive of losing even one loved one as the pain is so terrible. I had the incredible misfortune of losing three brothers, each passing about two months apart and then my mother six months later. The pain is truly indescribable. It felt like being hit by a tsunami and being completely wiped out. And then being hit again and again by giant waves before you even had a chance to recover from the first one.

Honestly, I don't even know how I survived that time. Well, I almost didn't. I lost 38 pounds and became severely dehydrated. I couldn't bring myself to eat or drink. All desire for living seemed to be taken out of me and I laid around as if in a vegetative state. Luckily I have wonderful friends who were very supportive during this time. When all this first happened they would take turns staying with me, cooking meals and keeping my place in good order.

One night I was visited by my brother Jim. Jim and I had always had a close connection and I recall him telling me at one point, that if anything happened to him that he would feel so sorry for me. He was always so protective of me, and I knew that it hurt him to think about me being alone without his help. I was in my bed when he came to me in that in that state between being awake and falling asleep. In fact, as I reflect back on it I'm not exactly sure if I was asleep or awake. But I do know that everything seemed very lucid and clear. As I was laying there all of a sudden I smelled him and it was like an intense, thick cloud washing over me. It smelled like a cloud of cigar smoke which had always been the sign that my brother Jim was entering the room. It wasn't often that you would see my brother without a cigar in his hand. He grinned at me a loving and warm smile and said, "They all sent me here because you need to quit hurting." Tears started rolling down my eyes, and I immediately felt held and comforted.

I asked him if I could hug him and he said "That is also why I am here, to hug you because you need it so bad." I reached out to him and he engulfed me in his arms. I felt him in a way that was real and tangible. It didn't feel like a dream or my imagination and it felt like his body was next to mine. It had texture and weight to it and more reality than just a spirit. After we had hugged for a little while he smiled and faded away. As he walked away from me, he turned sideways and kept his gaze on me but didn't turn his back.

I went to sleep with the most beautiful indescribable feelings. It was the first night in months that I had gotten some sleep. All the other nights up until that point I felt like I was always awake and vigilant just waiting for something to happen. I was finally able to eat and drink regularly and take care of myself as I had before. I got a haircut that I hadn't had in months and starting cleaning up the house. Now that I was able to take care of myself I could take care of my 90-year-old father who also was in need of a lot of help and caregiving.

After that night, I had other visitations from each of my brothers and my mother. But I must admit that my visitation from Jim was the most touching and had the most impact on me. The others sent clear messages to me. My oldest brother Charles told me that he is by my bed every night because he knows I am having trouble sleeping because my feet are burning and to please go to the doctor. The interesting thing was that it was true, my feet were burning, but I didn't tell anyone because I thought it was all in my head.

My brother George also came to me and said, "I love you. I never said it enough, but I do." It felt so good to have a sense of closure with my brother and how strange that that closure came not from this world but from the other side. My mother also came and visited me and said that she knew how cruel she was to me and that she was sorry and that she did love me. This also meant a lot to me as I felt that the relationship we had was filled with pain and I carried a lot of hurtful memories.

I feel like sometimes Jim flies by me shaped like a butterfly. It may seem odd, but it's an unyielding feeling that I get that his spirit is taking on the form of a butterfly. Once they all came shaped like butterflies, and I quickly took out my phone to capture it. I snapped photos with my phone as they kept appearing but when I went to look at the pictures, I could only see the flowers and no butterflies at all. All I could do was stand there crying, feeling so happy and comforted that they were still around me. This happened right before I went into the hospital to visit my dad and it took me awhile before I could stop crying. I didn't want my dad to be concerned about me, but I also wanted him to know that they were with him too.

At the time that all these visitations happened, I had been seeing a therapist to get through this tough time. I told him about every visit that I had, and he said that he was glad that I was open to experiencing their presence and that it was a beautiful thing to be able to realize that visitations are real. Without these visitations, I know without a doubt that I would not have survived this. Feeling their love, support and presence from the other side is the only thing that has kept me going. In this case, it was the dead that has kept me alive.

Change The Station

I recently lost a dear friend of mine. The empty hole that he left with his passing was filled with a tremendous burden of guilt. It's funny how when someone is alive we think they will be around forever, and we don't often feel grateful for their presence and treat them the way we should. I didn't always feel guilty, but at the time when he passed all those actions I regretted and held underground, came to the surface with a vengeance. Suddenly it was too late to change anything and all the things I had done and said were set in concrete forever. The thing is that I did love him a lot even though it didn't always come off that way.

I drive a truck for a living and spend long hours and many miles driving through what seems like endless space. At these times, the radio is often your best friend to get you through the loneliness. Well, shortly after my friend passed my radio station would regularly change from the country station to a Christian station. I never listened to the Christian station, and this had never happened before. It was annoying. I had no interest in hearing the Christian station.

After a few weeks of this, I mentioned it to the other driver that used my truck to see if he experienced the same strange thing. He is a country fan also, so I figured he would know. He looked at me, his face twisted and eyes drawn close together and said that no, this had never happened to him and that he didn't even know there was a Christian station. Upon hearing this, I immediately got an overwhelming feeling that my friend was trying to tell me something.

The guilt I was feeling seemed unbearable to me. Instead of diminishing, it only appeared to get worse with every passing day. It felt like my world was collapsing and I felt trapped in these thoughts like being locked in a small cage. I started talking to him in my truck. At first it began as a way to release the pressure valve and then it started to feel like my truck was a confessional box. I am sure that people thought I was crazy. I know my coworkers did. But I just kept talking, and I noticed the feelings of guilt slowly start to release. I told him that I was very sorry that I had treated him that way and that I missed him.

After about a month of this, the station changed. But not to the Christian station. It turned to an alternative rock station that was more his style of music and played a song from a local band. The song was about falling in love with the moment and carrying pain. It was about not taking the pain from the past into the present moment and enjoying each day for what it is. The lyrics in the song were so perfectly matched to what I was feeling and had been feeling for weeks.

I am still not entirely sure what the whole message is but I do know that it was him that was communicating with me and that he wanted me to know to let go of the guilt of the past and move on. From wherever he was, I believe that the guilt I was carrying must have seemed utterly pointless and unnecessary and that he didn't want me to hurt myself anymore. Even though I know that he wouldn't want me to feel guilty, I must admit that it's still hard for me. It is still a daily challenge to forgive myself and how I treated him.

Ever since that day when I heard that song, the radio station never changed channels again. I feel like once the message was communicated there was no need to keep doing that. I heard the message loud and clear from my friend. I am very thankful for his communication with me and am comforted knowing that he doesn't want me to feel sorry about anything. I feel that he is with me every day. I often see him in my dreams, and he has visited me and kissed me in my sleep. I am grateful that I have become aware of the signs that tell us that our loved ones are with us. Because now there is no longer any doubt in my mind that he has communicated with me and continued to be a part of my life. I may not be able to completely "change the station" with my feelings of guilt, but it is a comfort knowing he is by my side.

A Little While Longer

My wife Elizabeth was in very high spirits and chatting happily with me that morning. It was a welcome change as the last few weeks had been horrible for us, with the treatments that left her weak and a shadow of her former self. The prognosis was not good. Elizabeth only had a few more months to live, but I clung to the knowledge that we would be together for a little while longer.

Her packed bags were by the door of her hospital room, all ready for Elizabeth to come home. I could see that she was excited at having to go back home, and so was I. The house had been empty without Elizabeth's warm presence and I looked forward to having her there. Not that I didn't know how tough the months to come would be. Elizabeth would need round the clock care as she could do only a few things for herself.

None of that mattered. I had vowed to love and cherish her until death did us part, but more than that I just wanted more time with my Elizabeth. We had loved each other for forty years, raised children and we had been looking forward to growing old together. That would not be but we could fill the next few months with more happy memories and just talk and connect away from the hospital.

Our marriage had been blessed in that in all the forty years; our love had grown even stronger. I couldn't visualize my life without Elizabeth, but that was not a thought that I lingered on. She was coming home after months in the hospital, was all I thought. I had made all the necessary preparations to ensure that she would be as comfortable as possible.

We were waiting for the final discharge when suddenly Elizabeth's face paled and her breathing rhythm changed. Her hand flew to her chest and she gasped as though she couldn't breathe. I quickly rang the emergency bell and the room was flooded with medical personnel. I watched all these from the side, my heart thumping hard against my chest.

She passed on fifteen minutes after her breathing trouble started. I stared at her dead body disbelievingly. Her bag still waited by the door. I had trouble relating the cheery and talkative Elizabeth to one who was no more. I couldn't cry or even think. I just kept saying to myself that we had a few more months together, what had happened?

Our children, Susan and Henry, had just as hard a time adjusting to the news that their mother was gone.

They both worked and were looking forward to having their mother back home, even if it would be for only a few months. Now that chance to be with her was gone. None of us got the opportunity to say goodbye.

I called them from the hospital and they arrived about thirty minutes after Elizabeth had passed on. We left the hospital an hour later and not knowing what to do with ourselves we went to the park to try and make sense of what had happened. I had no comforting words for them as my own heart was twisted with pain.

My life seemed unfathomable and I had no idea how I would move on from there. I had not accepted that Elizabeth was going to leave us eventually. The time had not come to accept that truth but I knew that in the coming months I would slowly get used to the idea of Elizabeth gone. I felt as though someone had yanked my lifeline from my fingers and I now had nothing to hold on to.

We sat on the bench at the park and after a while we started speaking. We remembered Elizabeth and what a wonderful wife and mother she had been. By comforting each other, her death became a reality and though we felt immense sadness, it was a first step towards healing. We also spoke of practical matters relating to the next week and the things we needed to do.

After the park for well over three hours and then we all went to the house Elizabeth and I had shared for forty years. Her absence struck me as soon as I stepped into the front door and I wondered if I would carry the emptiness I felt for the rest of my life.

Though the house had been silent for all the time Elizabeth had been in the hospital, it had never seemed as lonely as it did that day. I suppose it was the knowledge that Elizabeth would never set foot in the house again.

My daughter Susan had Elizabeth's phone in her purse and she heard a beep. Puzzled she reached for the phone and we all gathered closer to Susan. The phone showed that there were three missed calls, all from the number 000-000-0000. My eyes welled up with tears. I knew the message was from Elizabeth.

She was letting us know that even though we had not had the time we had expected together, all was well. She was alright and I can't tell you how much comfort that gave me. The three of us looked at each other and we hugged. No words were needed as we all knew the calls were Elizabeth's way of connecting with us.

It has been tough getting through the grief but the knowledge that she is at peace keeps me going. There have been other signs from Elizabeth and though I miss her more than I can say, my heart is lighter from knowing that death is not the end of life. I love her so much and I know that our love extends beyond this world.

Thank you, Elizabeth, for giving me and our children one more moment with you. Your passing may not have been foreseen; however you have helped us from the other side by ensuring that we know that you're always with us.

Conclusion

Love never dies, my friend. Death is only a door to a new adventure, and as you've seen—and been inspired—by these stories, the signs are all around us!

Question: are you ready to start acknowledging the signs?

I hope so! If you are in any way unsure of what signs are real or imagined, I would urge you to get my free ebook Afterlife: 3 Easy Steps To Connecting And Communicating With Your Deceased Loved Ones as I know it will help you. It's FREE. No catch.

I hope you enjoyed this book. If so, please don't hesitate to review it as every single review helps spread the word.

If you'd like weekly inspiration, please visit my webpage at **www.BlairRobertson.com**

Of course, if you'd like me to share more stories, please drop me an email at blair@blairrobertson.com

Love and light to you. And remember, love never dies.

Blair Robertson

About The Author

Blair Robertson is a world-renowned psychic medium dedicated to demonstrating that love never dies, and that Spirit is all around us. Based in Phoenix, Arizona, he lives with his wife Wendy, the love of his life.

Blair has been featured on the Discovery Channel, Fox News, NBC, ABC, and hundreds of radio shows worldwide. He has produced a number of CDs, DVDs, and free online seminars on spiritual subjects.

Blair Robertson tours widely, giving demonstrations of communication with the afterlife. He was once branded a "comedium" by one of his fans for his sense of humor and compassion. Blair excels in delivering messages of love in a loving way.

He has a weekly inspirational newsletter, and we invite you to visit and subscribe at
www.BlairRobertson.com

Check out Blair's latest best-selling books by visiting Amazon.

Made in the USA
San Bernardino, CA
19 January 2020